Published in association with the
HAMPSHIRE CHRONICLE

WINCHESTER

THE POST-WAR YEARS

breedon **books**
PUBLISHING

Published in association with the
HAMPSHIRE CHRONICLE

WINCHESTER

THE POST-WAR YEARS

First published in Great Britain in 2002 by
The Breedon Books Publishing Company Limited
Breedon House, 3 The Parker Centre,
Derby, DE21 4SZ.

ISBN 1 85983 307 1

Printed and bound by Butler & Tanner, Frome, Somerset, England.
Cover printing by Lawrence-Allen Colour Printers, Weston-super-Mare,
Somerset, England.

CONTENTS

Acknowledgments

Our thanks to Karen Parker and the staff at the Historic Resource Centre, Winchester, for 'topping up' our picture collection. Thanks also to Steve Ridout, Frank Riddle, Terry Bond and Jon Macintosh for photographs. Finally our thanks to local historian Phil Yates for additional material and proof-reading.

Ordering pictures:

To inquire about ordering reprints of any of the pictures in this book, please telephone the Hampshire Chronicle on 01962 841772.

FOREWORD

WASHINGTON POST publisher Philip Graham described journalism as 'the first draft of history'. Newspapers may not always get it right but they are frequently the first to set down in writing news of an event. Hopefully, the *Hampshire Chronicle* has got it right more times than it has got it wrong in the paper's 230-year history. Since that first issue in August 1772, the paper has watched over the French Revolution, American Revolution, the Declaration of Independence by our American cousins, the Battle of Waterloo, Battle of Trafalgar, two world wars, countless Royal occasions, sporting events ranging from those early cricket matches at Hambledon to Southampton's 1976 FA Cup win. And it continues to record news week by week.

It has also photographed the news. Admittedly, the paper was hardly a pioneer in this respect. It wasn't until 1941 that the paper decided to indulge itself in the modern fashion of regularly producing photographs in the paper. Previously it had reserved this luxury for special occasions, such as Royal visits. And the pictures all appeared in a separate supplement to the paper.

Pictures may be worth a thousand words but they are unlikely to ever replace the written word completely. Even the birth of the talkies and television has failed to finish off newspapers. But pictures do have a special quality that sets them apart from words. A photograph can, on one level, accurately record who was standing where at a particular date and at a particular time. But on another level, it carries so much more information: the absolute joy on a child's face as she steps on stage to collect her first prize in a fancy dress competition; the hope of post-war Britons as they see houses being built in Winchester's suburbs; the eager anticipation as children dash down the road to play in winter's first fall of snow; or the sadness of a family mourning a loved one lost in tragic circumstances. All these emotions and more have been caught during the last 60 years by the photographers of the *Hampshire Chronicle*. Fortunately, unlike many photographic collections, these have survived.

Part of the reason they have survived lies in the unique make-up of the *Hampshire Chronicle*. For over 200 years it was a family-run newspaper and for much of the two centuries has resided in the same premises at 57 High Street, Winchester. Many documents and photographs have been stuffed in drawers and filing cabinets only to be found decades later. Others were stored more carefully in the walk-in safe that houses almost every copy of the *Chronicle* since 1772. But they have also survived because members of staff have realised the value in what they are producing not just as news to be thrown away a few days after it is printed but as that first draft of history. They have realised that while reporting and photographing events such as the cutting of the motorway through Twyford Down or the sinking of the *Titanic* that they are watching a momentous event in the county's history unfold before their eyes.

One major problem is ensuring that these pictures are correctly captioned, or that the right caption goes with the right picture. As the glass plates were stored away in boxes, little information was kept about each picture. After all, the photographer who took them knew what they were about and the plates had served their purpose. So as the glass plates were transferred on to computer, one of the biggest picture puzzles in history took place. Through the pages of the *Chronicle*, readers were urged to identify literally hundreds of pictures. Could they recall the event, the date, the names of the people? It's a never-ending quest, but of course readers loved nothing more than to pore over the pictures and identify who was who. Sometimes the toddler who had won first prize in fancy dress was able to recall that happy memory and at the same time solve another picture puzzle.

The struggle to preserve this heritage is not easy. Glass plates can easily shatter, old film can begin to 'dissolve' and even newsprint can become brittle and crumble away. The start of the 21st century has seen Winchester City Museum Services transfer these fragile assets onto computer. That's only a short-term solution. Even digital technology has a shelf-life and, an even bigger problem in this ever-changing world, is wondering if future generations will possess CD-Rom players to play back this information. The best we can do is pass our 'heritage baton' from our generation to the next generation and hope that, with each transfer of the information, only a small amount is lost each time.

What is certain is that the advent of the digital age means it is more important than ever before to capture history as it happens and preserve it for future generations.

Alan Cleaver
Editor
Hampshire Chronicle

THE BUILDING OF THE M3

The M3 Inquiry…

More than 20 years of inquiries, bitter debate and protest ended in 1994 with the full opening of the M3 link. The M3 Joint Action Group, composed of conservation bodies and others, fought the proposed cutting through Twyford Down in the High Court, at the European Commission, at public meetings, protests and demonstrations. Work on the motorway link began in September 1992, but protests, bad weather and construction difficulties delayed its progress. Hundreds of protesters lay down in the path of the diggers and several were arrested and jailed. Although defeated in their campaign, the protesters consoled themselves by claiming that the issue had raised public awareness nationwide about the damage to the environment arising from the government's road-building programme. The M3 Arrives… After the inquiry came the building of the motorway and its associated protests.

Before the M3… Memories of Winchester before the M3 extension – Hockley Junction pictured in 1982, a real bottle-neck at times.

Winchester bypass gave way to the M3 extension in 1994 but this picture from 1971 shows it in full flow. It has now been grassed over to its original state prior to 1938 when the bypass was constructed.

The M3 saga all began a quarter-of-a-century ago with the M3 Inquiry in Winchester, which expended zillions of man-hours and cost thousands of pounds. Resistance to the road was concerted and organised, with meetings and committees taking place across the city to discuss the myriad issues the huge scheme threw up. Inevitably – despite passionate pleas that such an historic and cultural city as Winchester should never be sullied by something as mundane as a motorway, the road went through – and the lawyers battened on all the fees. Prominent in this picture is city councillor, Lady Jennie Enfield, now Lady Bland, while the balding, bespectacled gentleman writing at lower left is the *Hampshire Chronicle* reporter Geoff Drake.

A protester makes an unusual stand against the M3 works.

Mud and desolation as the work progresses.

Hands across Twyford Down as a form of protest.

A torchlight procession through the newly cut extension.

Security men get to work.

And out you go!

Protesters in the trees find their perch doubly precarious as bulldozers move in.

Protesters on the march.

The banner men… making their point.

Jaw-jaw not war-war as protesters listen to arguments for and against the cutting.

David Croker, chairman of Twyford Down Association, with other protesters.

Outnumbered… A protester is carried away.

Protesters found anywhere to sit down and protest!

People from all walks of life took part in the Twyford Down fight.

Negotiating with the police.

More of a battlefield than a construction site.

Not the Somme but Twyford Down near Winchester.

A walking protest at Hockley junction brings traffic to a halt.

The view toward St Giles's Hill with All Saints' Church in the centre of the picture.

The protest attracted TV and other media.

Just a little diversion!

The long line and arm of the security forces.

IN ALL WEATHERS

All photographers love a good weather picture and the storm of 1990 provided some dramatic pictures such as this one in Andover Road, Winchester.

Snow galore outside Winchester Guildhall in January 1985.

The Great Storm of 1987 resulted in much damage to the landscape. This is the Andover Road north out of Winchester.

An act of God? A fallen tree during the 1987 storms in the grounds of Wolvesey Palace, home of the Bishop of Winchester.

Floods are now a regular part of our weather calendar. This scene shows Winchester's Recreation Park under flood in 2000.

Left abandoned, a city council recycling lorry. Excavations have shown that in the pre-Roman period a flood plain extended between Parchment and Union Streets which would have included the park area.

A Unigate Dairy milkman delivers the daily pint to a house in Park Avenue.

The appropriately named Water Lane which is close to the banks of the River Itchen.

The Deanery at Winchester Cathedral gains an extra quality with a fall of snow.

Winchester doesn't see much snow but it makes an occasional visit as in 1994 to Garnier Road.

Floods are nothing new as this picture of Bar End, Winchester, taken in the 1950s proves.

The fall of 1994 gave these folk crossing fields near Winchester College a novel mode of transport.

THE HAMPSHIRE CHRONICLE

The *Hampshire Chronicle* is the oldest newspaper in Hampshire, having been established in 1772. It has been at its offices at 57 High Street, Winchester since 1813. The presses at the offices closed in April 1991 and the paper is now printed at Southampton. However, the editorial and advertising still work out of the High Street offices – a building that contains plenty of history (and a ghost!).

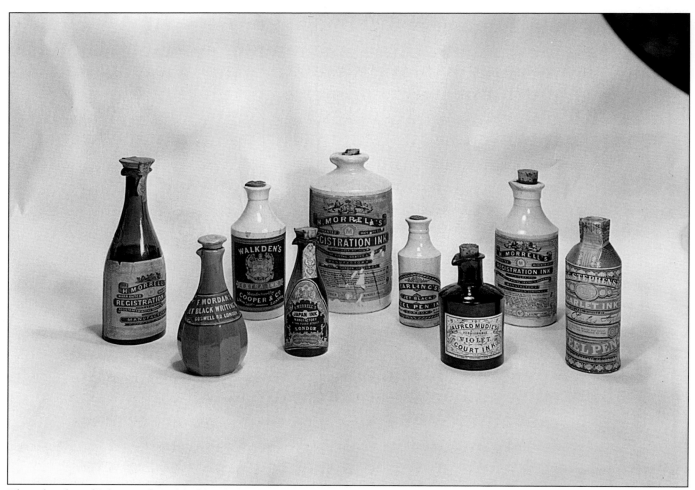

These bottles of ink were found hidden behind a wooden panel in the reception of the *Hampshire Chronicle* offices at 57 High Street in the 1940s. A workman lent a bit too heavily on a wooden panel and his elbow broke through the wood to reveal the bottles of ink. In the 19th century the *Chronicle* sold bottles of ink along with books and other paraphenalia and it is believed the bottles were deliberately hidden to be discovered at some point in the future. The bottles are now on display in a cabinet in the reception area of the newspaper office.

Jack Rawlins (left) and Sidney (Olly) Holloway on the stone of the *Hampshire Chronicle* in the 1970s. In the background is Bill Loveland who joined the company in 1922. The pages being made up could weigh up to 2cwt and were sent down to the press room at that time by hand-operated hoist. These offices – at 57 High Street, Winchester – are now the home of the reporters for the *Hampshire Chronicle*.

The *Hampshire Chronicle* has published every week since 1772 but a little bit of promotion never did anyone any harm and here the Winchester local paper can be seen at a show selling its wares.

The *Hampshire Chronicle* offices

The following pictures show the good old days of Winchester's local paper, the *Hampshire Chronicle*, when the photographs were etched on to plates and the printing press still thundered away at the High Street premises. Today the photographers use digital cameras, the reporters use computers and the paper is printed at Southampton.

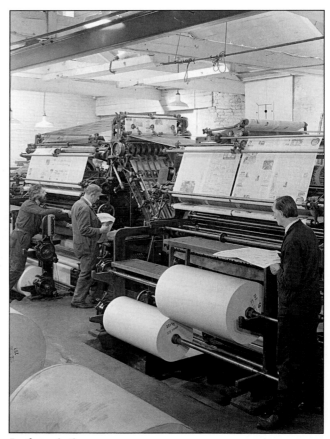

In the printing room.

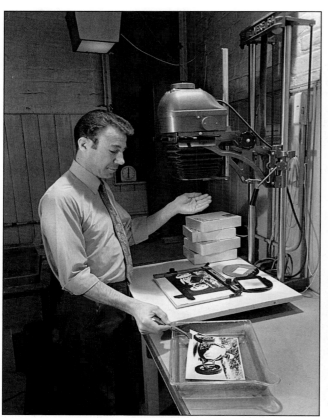

Photographer Roy Knight developing a photograph.

Photographer George Walsh studies this contraption.

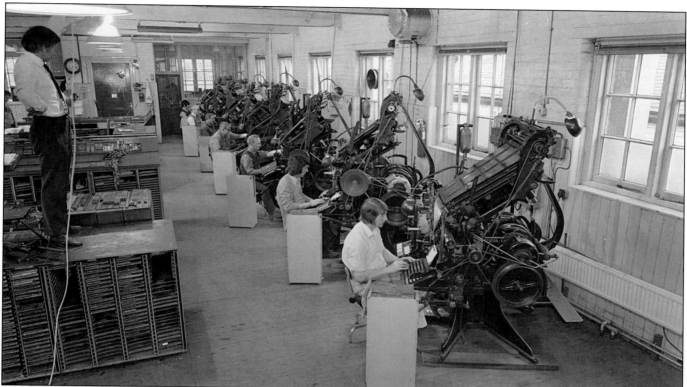

Busy at the lithograph machines.

Not bad – Roy Knight looks at his results.

FROM THE AIR

An aerial photograph of Winchester looking north with Winchester Cathedral on the right hand of the picture. The barracks and the new county council offices are in the centre of the picture taken in the early 1960s.

An aerial photograph (facing west) of Winchester taken in the early 1960s with the new county council offices at the top of the picture.

An aerial photograph (looking west toward Stockbridge Road) of Winchester taken in the early 1960s. The new county council offices are at the bottom left of the picture and Winchester City railway station top centre.

WINCHESTER CATHEDRAL

Bishop John Taylor in Winchester Cathedral, 1975.

Lime trees are felled outside Winchester Cathedral.

The once glorious avenue leading up to Winchester Cathedral.

How the mighty are fallen – the demise of the lime tree avenue outside Winchester Cathedral – however, new trees have now been planted. The flint building in the background is the City Museum opened in 1903, one of the first purpose-built museums in the country outside London.

Cathedral Close in the snow, looking towards Cheyney Court.

Bishop Michael Scott-Joynt at Winchester Cathedral.

Bishop John Taylor outside the Cathedral in his enthronement procession, 8 February 1975.

WINCHESTER COLLEGE

Winchester College War Memorial Cloister re-dedication ceremony, 14 November 1948. Lord Wavell is pictured giving the address. Behind him are the Bishop of Winchester and the College Chaplains.

Winchester College war memorial cloister re-dedication ceremony on Sunday 14 November 1948.

Winchester College War Memorial Cloister re-dedication ceremony, Sunday 14 November 1948. Pictured are Lord Wavell, the headmaster and warden of Winchester College.

ROYAL VISITS AND EVENTS

Princess Anne meets St John Ambulance Cadets outside Winchester Cathedral.

Diana, Princess of Wales, meets the Winchester crowds in 1992.

The Queen Mother on a visit to Hillier gardens in 1978 with Sir Harold and Lady Hillier.

The Queen hands out Maundy money at Winchester Cathedral in March 1979.

Princess Diana on a visit to Winchester in 1992 is photographed on the Guildhall steps.

Princess Diana in Winchester.

The final parade of the Hampshire Regiment through Winchester. The regiment amalgamated with the Queen's Regiment in 1992 to form the Princess of Wales's Royal Regiment (Queen's and Royal Hampshires). See next two pages also.

Previous page and above: The Queen and Prince Philip on a visit to Winchester in 1982.

The Queen, accompanied by the Mayor, Councillor Mrs F.S. Thackeray, meets Winchester schoolchildren at Wolvesey playing fields during her official visit to Winchester on 25 May 1955.

The Queen arrives at Winchester railway station to visit the newly-formed Royal Green Jackets in July 1967.

HM Queen Elizabeth II chats to one of her loyal followers when she opened the new visitors' centre at Winchester Cathedral on the morning of 19 November 1993. After lunch she opened the new Hampshire Record Office in Sussex Street.

Lord Mountbatten visits training ship *Mercury* on the banks of the Hamble for an inspection and to hand out prizes to the cadets. TS *Mercury* trained cadets for the Royal and Merchant Navys before closing in 1968.

The Duchess of Kent's visit to Winchester College, 24 March 1949.

The Duchess of Kent's visit to Winchester College, 24 March 1949.

HRH Princess Elizabeth and HRH the Duke of Edinburgh on Sunday 23 November 1947 in the grounds of Broadlands, near Romsey.

The royal honeymoon – HRH Princess Elizabeth and HRH the Duke of Edinburgh on Sunday 23 November 1947 in the grounds of Broadlands, near Romsey, where they spent part of their honeymoon. The couple are looking at photographs of their wedding.

Earl Mountbatten of Burma, High Steward of Romsey, inspects the men of the 4th and 5th Battalions of The Royal Hampshire Regiment when the regiment was granted the Freedom of Romsey in September 1959. Earl Mountbatten is accompanied by Brigadier G.D. Browne, Colonel of the Regiment.

The Queen visits the newly-formed Green Jackets in 1967.

A royal visit to Romsey in 1957.

Romsey is home to the Mountbatten family and royal events are a regular occurrence. This picture shows the reception for newly-weds Lord and Lady Brabourne. Pictured left to right: Pamela Mountbatten (sister of bride), Princess Margaret, unknown, Lord Mountbatten, Queen Elizabeth (the Queen Mother), Lord and Lady Brabourne, King George VI, Countess Mountbatten, Princess Elizabeth, Mr Oliver Hoare.

Diana, Princess of Wales, on a visit to Winchester in 1992.

The Queen goes walkabout in Winchester in 1979 much to the delight of the crowds.

A big cheer for the Queen from this crowd in 1979 at Winchester.

Diana, Princess of Wales, shows why she was so well loved.

The Queen and Prince Philip complete with Beefeaters at Winchester Cathedral accompanied by the Dean of Winchester, the Right Revd Michael Stancliffe.

The Queen Mother is greeted by school children while on a visit to St Cross, near Winchester, in 1986 on the 850th anniversary of the founding of the country's oldest almshouses.

The Queen's silver jubilee in 1977 was celebrated with a huge street party in Alresford.

Prince Charles is given a dignified welcome to Winchester.

Coronation Day 1953 and Bishop's Waltham's carnival queen and princesses are cheered on by the crowd. This picture was taken in the ruins of the Palace which dates from the 12th century.

Bramdean's Coronation Day street party with children tucking in to the sandwiches and cakes.

The death of Princess Diana in 1997 resulted in an astonishing display of public grief. Broadlands at Romsey formed a focal point for tributes as Diana and Charles had stayed at the Mountbatten's home for a short time after their wedding.

The Queen's Coronation in 1953 and the whole country was celebrating – including Granville Place, Winchester. The two men and the woman standing by their front doors on the left of the picture are Mr Chris McDonald, Mr Len Savey and his wife, Ada. Other families present are the Browns, the Barretts, the Hedleys, the Harpers, the Masters, the Goldings and the Cowdreys. The mayor of Winchester judged the fancy dress and the winner was Christine Cowdrey, second was Patsy McDonald and third was her brother, Chris McDonald. Bill Beaumont brought his piano onto the street and kept everyone entertained throughout the day.

MILITARY CONNECTIONS

Serle's House in Southgate Street, Winchester, has been the home of The Royal Hampshire Regiment since 1881 and boasts this superb staircase designed by architect Thomas Archer. Built in the 1730s as a private house for the Sheldon family, the house was sold to Winchester attorney, James Serle, in 1781. His son, Peter, served with the Hampshire Militia during the Napoleonic wars, and used the house at his headquarters. In 1881, the Militia became the 3rd Battalion of The Hampshire Regiment. Peter Serle later sold the house to the government to ensure its continuance as the headquarters of the county regiment. In 2001 Hampshire County Council bought the house from the Ministry of Defence to save it from development. It now contains the Regimental Museum and the Regimental Memorial Garden.

The illustrious history of The Royal Hampshire Regiment was honoured by the opening and dedication of the Memorial Garden and Regimental Museum at Serle's House by the Lord Lieutenant of Hampshire, the Duke of Wellington, and the Bishop of Winchester, Dr Mervyn Haig. The regiment's Roll of Honour in Winchester Cathedral was dedicated on the same day.

Left: The parade ground at the former Peninsula Barracks, Winchester, where generations of soldiers did their 'square bashing'. It was also a venue for military displays including the popular annual Sounding the Retreat spectacular. The building in the background is the Short Block completed in 1904 to replace the King's House burned down in 1894. It was turned into barracks for the British Army during the Napoleonic wars. Four regimental museums are still housed in the old barracks complex – The Royal Green Jackets, opened by HM the Queen in 1989, the Gurkhas, the Royal Hussars and the Light Infantry.

Below: The guardroom at the main entrance to the former Peninsula Barracks incorporates some of the designs by Sir Christopher Wren for the King's House in the Barracks Square. The pillared guardroom is now a listed building.

ON PARADE

Winchester Cathedral has, over the centuries, been host to many parades. On this occasion it was the turn of Brownies to make their way for a special service.

This procession through Winchester High Street captures some long lost shops from the city centre including Dunn & Co and Timothy White's chemist.

Winchester churches unite for the annual Good Friday procession of Christian witness through the city centre. This procession pictured in the mid-1970s is led by (left to right) Monsignor Sidney Mullarkey, parish priest of St Peter's Catholic Church; Dr John Taylor, Bishop of Winchester; and Methodist minister, Revd Wallace White.

The City Champion was an office held in Winchester even up to the 1960s. Here the City Champion leads a procession through Westgate, Winchester.

Civic parades always attract crowds. This one is wending its way through The Square to Winchester's Cathedral.

Young people from all branches of the services have often had the honour to march along Winchester's streets to mark special days or events. Seen above and in the next three pictures are parades in Jewry Street.

And we finish this chapter with five pictures of Scouts on parade – complete with short trousers and wide-brimmed hats. Fortunately fashions do change and today's scouts have a more cool image.

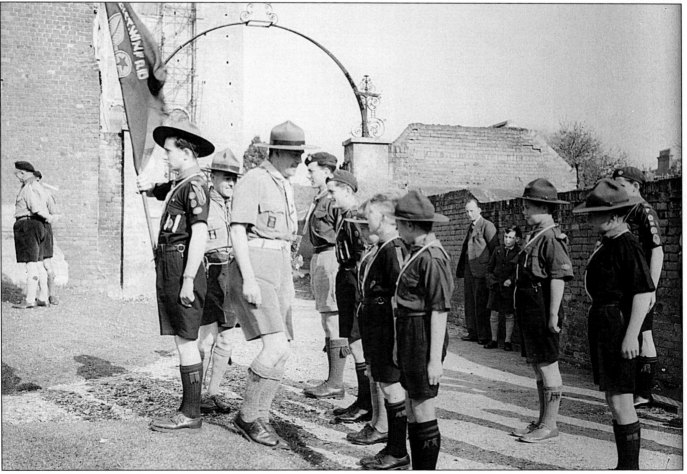

TRADITIONS

On March 25 (Lady Day) the annual Tichborne Dole is distributed to the villagers of Tichborne, Cheriton and Lane End. The custom dates back some 900 years to honour the death wish of Lady Isabella Tichborne who begged her husband for a gift of land whose yield would provide the poor of the parish with a yearly dole of bread. Her callous husband said she could have as much land as she could crawl round carrying a blazing torch. Although dying, Lady Isabella managed to crawl round some 23 acres. She swore that the Tichborne family would be cursed if it ever discontinued the dole. It was abolished in 1796, but the disasters that followed forced the family to revive the custom.

At the Hospital of St Cross, near Winchester, travellers can still call and ask for the Wayfarers Dole of bread and beer – a tradition that has been in existence for centuries.

HAMPSHIRE AT WORK

Peninsula Barracks, Winchester, provided an ideal setting for Hampshire firefighters to demonstrate their speed and expertise. The majority of the buildings in these pictures have now been converted into luxury residential apartments.

Hampshire at work.

Charcoal burners at work in the New Forest.

Watercress has for many years been an important industry in Hampshire, Alresford being the most famous town for the growing of this plant.

Hurdle makers at work near Winchester.

Men at work in 1959 in the newly-opened Elizabeth II Court building of Hampshire County Council.

Southampton docks has provided essential employment and industry to the county of Hampshire. Here QEI docks at the King George V dock in Southampton.

The fashions give away the 1960s date in this picture of Midland Bank in Eastleigh.

Hyde Abbey Motor Works in Winchester. A motor dealer existed on this site until the end of the 20th century before giving way to much needed new homes, known as Silchester Close.

Wykeham Motors' building was in Station Hill near the current location of the county record office. Many a young Winchester motorist would have snapped up the latest model from these premises.

Romsey Road School in 1956 when work was under way on the building of a school swimming pool.

Taverns and Shops

The Albion remains today in Winchester's Stockbridge Road but the Eagle Hotel, Andover Road, has been converted to flats known as Eagle Court.

The Crown Hotel on the corner of Jewry Street and North Walls, Winchester, pictured in 1974. A new office block stands here.

The Dolphin Inn that stood on the corner of St Thomas Street and High Street, Winchester. If you look closely today you can still see the name on the building and figures of dolphins over the doorway, but otherwise it has been converted to shops and offices.

The Georgian window above the Hammond Bros. shop in Jewry Street (now Arrow News) was once part of the original Winchester Theatre built in 1785. This collapsed during the demolition of the adjoining properties in 1982. The window has been rebuilt to the same design with the sign of The Phoenix above the new arch.

The Empire Meat Company's shop at 115 High Street, Winchester *c*.1950–2. Whittards, tea and coffee specialist shop, now occupy the premises.

The Oriel Hotel in City Road, Winchester, no longer exists but this picture of the hotel's cellar bar may bring back some memories.

Winchester's Exchange pub remains a popular place for a bite to eat and a drink. Here it is in early days and looking very smart.

The eastern side of Winchester's Andover Road pictured in March 1974. Capital House now stands here.

The Whitwams music shop in the High Street, Winchester, provided all the best music equipment in Winchester from 1909 to 1999. This is their showroom pictured in the 1960s with joint proprietor David Harding and a potential customer.

The former John Waters Deli, in High Street, Winchester, now part of Dixons.

Winton Court Hotel sadly no longer exists but used to stand in Southgate Street, Winchester. This is the cellar bar. The property is now part of Devenish House.

Bernfeld's sumptuous display on the top floor of God Begot House, High Street, Winchester. The historic building, dating from the 16th century, is now home to Ask Pizza. This area in the 11th century was known as 'God begeaton' meaning 'good bargain'.

It's hard to imagine a town without a Woolworths but the company pulled out of Winchester some years back, giving up their High Street store. This photograph, however, shows the rear entrance to the store from St George's Street.

Whitwams music shop occupied this site for nearly 100 years. The business still operates in Winchester but this store closed at the end of the 20th century and is now Fox & Sons, estate agents.

Bernfelds Shop (ground floor) in the God Begot House, Winchester.

Two scenes of God Begot House, Winchester. One showing it during its time as Bernfeld Brothers jewellery store and the other as Richoux Restaurant. It is now Ask Pizza. In 1052 Queen Emma, mother of Edward the Confessor, bequeathed 'The Manor of God Begot' to the Priory of St Swithun. After the Reformation the manor became the property of the Dean and Chapter of the Cathedral and remained so until 1866 when it was sold.

October 1991 is the date of this picture of Andover Road, Winchester. This part of town near the railway station remains a lively shopping area. Bridger, the locksmiths, has traded here for over 30 years.

Chesil Rectory stands the test of time, dating from 1459 and is currently used as a restaurant.

The Carfax Hotel on Station Hill in Winchester 1971. The site is now occupied by the Hampshire Record Office opened by HM the Queen on 19 November 1993.

Many a reader may have had their car repaired at the Gordon Holland garage on City Road, Winchester. This picture was taken in 1974. The building is now divided between Chessington Tyres and Carpets and Curtains.

The corner of Jewry Street and City Road, Winchester in 1974.

The Railway Tavern that once stood on Station Hill, Winchester.

ON THE RAILWAY

Eastleigh goods sidings. Eastleigh was the railway capital of the south and has provided the area with valuable employment over the years.

The last passenger train for Newbury and Didcot leaves Chesil Station, Winchester on 7 March 1960.

For a period during the summers of 1959, 1960 and 1961 the Saturday-only Southampton to Winchester diesel service was diverted to Chesil Station, so reducing congestion at Winchester's mainline station.

The Pines Express diverted to the Chesil line at Winchester, possibly because of works on the main line, in 1960. By this time the line was closed to passenger traffic and the canopies of the up-platform of Chesil Station had already been removed.

A passenger train pulling into the down-platform at Sutton Scotney.

The now defunct station at Sutton Scotney in the glory days of steam.

The Sprat and Winkle line – with Horsebridge Station looking rather deserted in this 1966 picture. The line is now the site of the Test Way footpath.

The final day of the Meon Valley Railway which ran from Alton to Fareham and closed in 1955.

A shunter at Winchester City in October 1963, known affectionately by locals as Puffing Billy.

Chesil Station in December 1962, used by this time for freight traffic only.

The *Mallard* passes through Winchester in 1962. This famous engine is now housed in the Railway Museum at York.

All aboard for a steam special in 1963. *The Flying Scotsman* hauling the Isle of Wight Special passing through Winchester City station.

BUILDING OUR FUTURE

The demand for housing at the end of World War Two saw
large new developments on the city boundaries. Work began
on the second stage of the Stanmore estate (pictured) in
1946 with additions to Highcliffe in 1948. New estates were
built at Weeke and Winnall, and the large new estate of
private houses at Badger Farm was started in the 1970s.

The late 1950s and early 1960s saw the building of the law courts near Westgate, Winchester. The courts are now second only to
the Old Bailey and have housed many famous trials including that of Rosemary West.

St Georges Street after widening had been completed around 1957. At the top of the street at its junction with Jewry Street, the George Hotel had been demolished and work had just been started on the Barclays Bank building. Note the traffic was still all one-way – only down instead of up – as today.

The 1,000th home to be built by Winchester Rural District Council is handed over to the tenant in September 1951.

The former Salvation Army Citadel in Parchment Street, Winchester, prior to its rebuilding.

With the Chesil railway station closed and the tunnel shut off, there was an opportunity to give the city a much-needed car park. This picture shows the building of the car park in 1985.

St Swithun-upon-Kingsgate undergoes restoration in the late 1970s. In mediaeval days it was not uncommon for churches to be built over city gates and there were three in Winchester. This tiny church, dating from the 13th century, is the only one to survive. It is now combined with St Lawrence-in-the-Square Church.

Stanmore in 1975 and more houses are built for the city's growing population.

Easton Lane, Winchester had a new roundabout in 1995 to cope with traffic using the nearby M3 junction and Tesco superstore.

Toward the end of the 20th century the Theatre Royal in Winchester closed down but has now been beautifully restored and is once again hosting big names from the arts world.

St Paul's Hospital, Winchester (originally a 19th-century workhouse), in October 1987. The building has now been converted to flats.

The building of Sir John Moore barracks, near Winchester, which took the place of the Penninsula barracks.

Above: The city centre car park being cleared to make way for the Brooks shopping centre (pictured below) which open in February 1991. Roman and mediaeval finds were made here.

Winchester may be a historic city but new buildings are added all the time. The Brooks shopping centre gave new life in the early 1990s to a part of Winchester that had previously existed as a car park.

The Theatre Royal, Winchester, was closed for six years at the end of the 20th century but has now been refurbished and is once again hosting arts events. This picture was taken in the early 1970s when the building was a cinema, used as such from 1920 to 1974.

Andover Road in 1978 with the buildings on the eastern side demolished. Albert Court residential flats for the elderly were erected here.

Bar End, Winchester in the 1970s.

Winchester railway station in 1977 as work got under way on improving the access route.

The Cricketers pub and Jno Steel undertakers immediately places this as the Bridge Street roundabout in Winchester but the Hampshire Auto building has been demolished and offices built in their place.

Sussex Street, Winchester in 1978 with the building of the underpass. The new county record office was built on land to the right of this picture.

Another view of Sussex Street, Winchester, looking north, with the land on the left being cleared for the new County Record Office.

WINCHESTER AT LEISURE

Why do the British love pram races so much? Certainly these revellers near Winchester seem to be enjoying every moment of this bizarre English sport.

The river flowing through Winchester has always provided sport and entertainment, such as this canoe gala in the Recreation Park.

Alresford's popular Donkey Derby pictured in the mid 1960s during the town's annual carnival at Alrebury Park. Leading the field is Tony Curtis of Alresford.

The Tour de France also did a tour of the south of England in 1994 and took in Winchester High Street where thousands lined the streets to view the spectacle.

The silver screen was wooing children as far back as 1951 when, as this picture shows, they queued for the latest blockbuster. On this occasion it was *Kim*, starring Errol Flynn, at the Odeon in North Walls, Winchester. The building next door to the cinema was the art school, formerly built for St Swithun's School.

The Odeon, North Walls, Winchester, in May 1970. The cinema no longer exists and The Screen in Southgate Street is the only 'silver screen' in the city today. The Odeon site is now occupied by the Richard Moss House retirement homes.

Flower and vegetable shows remain popular today. This particularly proud show was held at the Guildhall, Winchester in 1948.

A vintage car rally at the Rifle Range, Chilcomb provides plenty of interest to visitors.

September 1999 saw archaeologists once more looking for the elusive remains of King Alfred believed to be buried near Winchester. The hunt centred around River Park Leisure Centre but was not to be successful on this occasion.

The late 1940s or early 1950s is the possible date of Winchester chess players contemplating their next moves.

Previous page and above: Flower shows always provide an opportunity for pretty pictures that combine the best in arrangements with the best in fashion.

A tablespoon of rum helped Hyde United FC win the Northbrook Cup in the 1947–48 season. The final against the Hampshire Depot was played on a snow and ice-bound pitch on 21 February 1948. Before the game Tom Maugham, landlord of the King Alfred Inn, gave the Hyde team a tablespoon of rum which they swear helped them beat the Depot team by 3 goals to 2. Hyde United were also Winchester and District League champions in the same season. Back row (left to right): H. Palmer, A. Webb, A. Alborough (captain), D. Green, A. House, C. Ricquier, F. Vidow (reserve). Front row: R. Patience, N. Alexander, F. Muspratt, L. Hutchings, P. Thompson.

Winchester hosts the annual folk festival – here Woodfidley Folk Dancers entertain in Market Street.

Sport has always played an important part in Winchester life and rugby has often been as popular as football.

The crib in St Thomas's Church, Winchester proved a magical attraction to these children. The church in Southgate Street is now the St Thomas Centre.

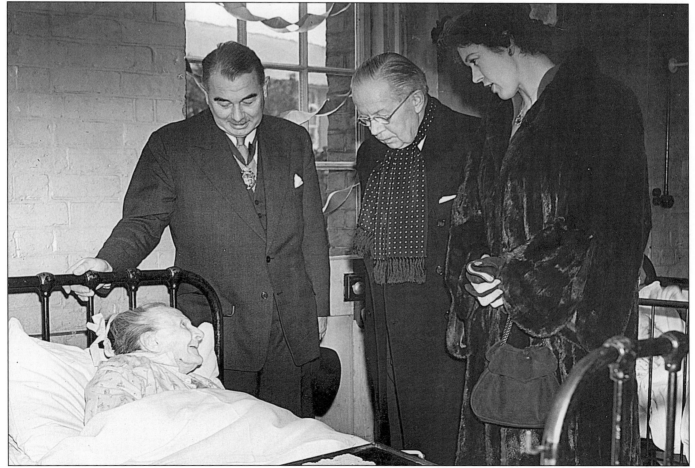

The mayor of Winchester traditionally visits those unfortunate enough to be in hospital at Christmas. This picture was taken at the old St Paul's hospital in Winchester.

Previous page and above: Everyone loves a party and this Christmas party at Stanmore Nursery, Winchester no doubt generated many happy memories for those children who took part in the early 1950s.

The *News of the World* organised a number of darts tournaments. This one was held in Winchester's Guildhall in the late 1940s.

Christmas is a time for singing carols outdoors – whatever the weather. Fortunately for these revellers in Wickham in the early 1950s, the weather seems to have been fine if a little cold.

Cricket has been played on Broadhalfpenny Down opposite the Bat and Ball Pub at Hambledon since 1750, giving the village a strong claim to being 'the cradle of cricket'. The present Hambledon Cricket Club celebrated its 250th anniversary in 2000 with a cricket week which included a match against the MCC. Here members show how the game was played when the club was in its infancy.

Hampshire has always been – and remains – a home for horse lovers and for the racing of horses. Winchester had its own racecourse in the 19th century at Worthy Down. Edward VII, as Prince of Wales, enjoyed the races here accompanied by his mistress, Lillie Langtry.

COUNTRY MATTERS

A hunting we will go. In the days before hunt protests, the Hursley Hunt sets out from the gates of Hursley Park.

The Itchen with St Catherine's Hill in the background in 1994.

The picturesque River Test near Stockbridge. The river is claimed to be the finest trout stream in the world.

Beaulieu Road horse sales in the New Forest ensure that the Forest's way of life continues.

Jim Lane, hurdle maker, of Winchester demonstrates his craft.

Hambledon – and not a protester in sight!

Hursley hounds on an outing at Broadlands, near Romsey.

The popularity of ploughing matches has never waned and the skill of the farmer is here clearly demonstrated.

Previous page and above: Hampshire has always been proud of its ploughing tradition and annual ploughing matches ensure standards don't slip!

Country crafts such as hurdle-making always prove popular at Hampshire shows.

CROP CIRCLES

Aliens, freek whirlwinds or hoaxers? We may never know but these Hampshire crop circles still make for some remarkable photographs, some of them appearing in fields at Cheesefoot Head on the road to Petersfield.

AROUND WINCHESTER

The village of Meonstoke – delightful at any period in its history.

Lyndhurst in days before the tourists discovered its secrets! William the Conqueror made the town the administrative centre when he created the New Forest in 1079.

This picture of Wherwell (usually pronounced 'Werral') could have been taken any time during the last 100 years as the village has hardly changed (thank goodness!). But it's thought this picture dates from the early 1950s.

Unmistakeably Farley Mount, just west of Winchester which, standing nearly 600ft above sea level, offers extensive views across Hampshire and, on a good day, the Isle of Wight. Visitors to the hill, known as Mount Down, will discover that the monument and barrow are a grave and memorial to a remarkable horse. The inscription tells the story: 'Underneath lies buried a horse, the property of Paulet St John Esq, that in the month of September 1733 leaped into a chalk pit twenty-five feet deep afoxhunting with his master on his back and in October 1734 he won the Hunters Plate on Worthy Downs and was rode by his owner and was entered in the name of "Beware Chalk Pit".'

Car accidents have existed as long as the car but fortunately this one at Pitt didn't look too serious.

Romsey market place in the early 1960s. Malting and brewing were the main industries here.

Romsey town centre modernised with a roundabout around Lord Palmerston's statue. But some motorists are still known to park there!

Romsey market place before its conversion to a roundabout. Matthew Noble's bronze statue of Lord Palmerston dominates the area. Palmerston, born and brought up at Broadlands, later the home of Lord Mountbatten, was Prime Minister 1855–8.

All roads lead to Chilbolton, pictured in 1977, on the south bank of the River Test.

Despite the vintage car, this picture was taken in Chawton as late as 1973. Jane Austen's former home, where she wrote the novels *Mansfield Park*, *Emma* and *Persuasion*, is on the left. She moved from Chawton to Winchester a short while before her death in 1817, and is buried in the cathedral.

Waiting for the school bus at Chawton, one mile south of Alton and now free from heavy traffic following the opening of the bypass.

King's Infant School, Chandler's Ford, pictured in 1990. The town is known as the halfway point between Winchester and Southampton. There is a pub in the centre called The Halfway Inn.

Careful as you go… Colden Common children on their way to school.

Colden Common School. Colden Common is a small village between Twyford and Fair Oak and has grown considerably in recent years with the increase in residential estates.

Stockbridge with the historic Grosvenor Hotel on the right.

Twyford Pump Station remains in good working order thanks to the support of enthusiasts. Here it is pictured on an open day in 1988. Fred Dibnah, former steeplejack and TV personality, makes regular guest appearances here on open days.

Hursley village. Quiet at the best of times but soon to be even quieter if the planned 30mph limit goes ahead. John Keble, after whom Keble College, Oxford, was named, was vicar here 1836–66.

Bishop's Waltham town centre pictured in 1978. In the 19th century the town had its own bank.

Broad Street, Alresford in 1992. Novelist Mary Russell Mitford was born in this street in 1787.

West Street, Alresford. At the top of this street on the right-hand side is the southern terminus station of the Mid-Hants Railway, which runs 10 miles to Alton. The railway is affectionately known as The Watercress Line.

THIS AND THAT

The Geoffrey de Havilland memorial plaque at Seven Barrows, near Litchfield. It was here that the aviation pioneer carried out his first flight in a homemade aeroplane in September 1910, one of the milestones in Hampshire's aviation history which includes the Schneider Trophy air races in the 1920s and 1930s and the testing and manufacture of the Battle of Britain Spitfires.

Election time and Peter Smithers (who was Tory MP for Winchester from 1950 to 1964) was out gaining support in St John Street, Winchester. The man in the centre of the picture, to the left of the horse, is Joseph Young. He worked for Bill Passey, who is sitting on the cart in the background. Bill owned a knacker's business in Winchester and a stables in Lower Brook Street. The horse we can see was called Dolly and the one pulling the cart with the Peter Smithfield sign was called Robert. Mr Smithers lived in Colebrook Street and was also an enthusiastic orchid grower. The lady with the knotted head scarf is Mrs Wilson.

Since the day the motor car arrived in Winchester, there have also been accidents. And newspapers like the *Hampshire Chronicle* have reported these mini-dramas. Even today the newspaper reports on even minor accidents involving the motor car. This particular crash occurred at the junction of St John's Road and Alresford Road in Winchester. The fire service are on hand not so much to put out a fire but to help cut injured motorists free from the wreckage. Note the King Alfred bus in the background – On New Year's Day every year these vintage buses can be seen being driven once more around Winchester by enthusiasts for those good old days.

Winchester Crown Court hosts some of Britain's biggest criminal trials and therefore attracts much media attention. Here photographers try to capture a picture of Rose West as she arrives at the court.

Fire at Winchester's Guildhall in 1969 – but fortunately it was extinguished before all of this wonderful building was destroyed. This extension to the Guildhall was built in 1875 on the site of the old police station.

Who in Winchester will ever forget the election of 1997? Lib-Dem candidate Mark Oaten beat the former Tory MP Gerry Malone by just two votes. The result was challenged in court and there was a re-run six months later. This time Mark Oaten won by an astonishing 21,556 majority.

Sadly the reason for all these children gathering in this council yard is forgotten but we couldn't let this cracking picture go to waste.

The Assize Court used to sit inside Winchester's Great Hall as this picture of 1952 shows. Today the Crown Court has its own building next door and the Great Hall remains a home to the Round Table.

The Victoria Hospital, Alresford Road, Winchester, is another well-known landmark that has recently disappeared from the landscape. Lee House Hospital now occupies the site.

Staple Gardens, Winchester, looks a lot better these days than this 1978 picture recalls.

A fierce fight by the people of Winchester saved the delightful Mildmay vets building in the centre of Winchester. It had once been a pub and its 'silent clock' on the front of the building recalled the days when new laws stopping landlords giving customers loans 'on tick'.

The scene is easily recognisable as Bridge Street, Winchester on the east of the city but none of these stores remain. The Old Mill restaurant is now Pizza Express, Knitcraft is Printed Page and W. Taylor's is currently unoccupied.

The north-east corner of Winchester with Spitfire Bridge and the Winchester bypass photographed in the early 1960s. The bridge was made famous by the stunt of a World War Two pilot reputed to have flown his Spitfire under it. The story says the plane clipped the bridge on its way through leaving part of its wing tip behind. The bridge was demolished in 1983 to make way for the M3 motorway extension.

Brought to light after 700 years, this mosaic floor was unearthed at the site of the Roman Villa at Sparsholt. Dated about AD 300, the floor was restored and relaid in Winchester City Museum in May 1969.

'Gee… is this Camelot?' cried an American tourist when she visited Winchester's Great Hall and the famous Round Table. Well, not really, madam. Although Winchester is one of the favoured sites for King Arthur's legendary Camelot, the Great Hall is all that remains of a castle built after the Norman Conquest. Henry III rebuilt the present hall in 1222. In the 1970s, radiocarbon tests dated the Round Table between 1250 and 1280 and may have been commissioned by Henry III. Some experts think the oak table was ordered by Edward I during a revival of interest in the Arthurian legend. Whatever the origin, the table is a magnificent sight and one of the city's much-loved symbols.

In safe hands. An officer from the Hampshire branch of the British Red Cross comforts a baby evacuee from Tristan da Cunha. The island was threatened by volcanic eruptions in 1962 and the whole population evacuated to Calshot in Hampshire. Some of the refugees were accommodated in houses lent by the New Forest District Council and others given temporary homes with local residents. Founded in 1909, the Hampshire Red Cross has looked after the wounded and displaced from two world wars and provided havens for post-war refugees from the Hungarian uprising in 1956 and the Vietnamese Boat People in 1973.

Hampshire's thriving Junior Red Cross cadets at their annual Youth and Junior Day at the county headquarters at Weeke Manor, where they give demonstrations of their skills and enjoy sports, camp fires and craft activities.

The old dining hall at Twyford School. Originally the room had been built as a school room by Dr Kitchin, the headmaster, in 1858. The refectory table is still in use and has the date 1652 carved upon it.

No doubting the date or place – we'll just add it was taken in August of that year.

Archaeology has always been an important part of the historic city of Winchester. Here a dig takes place in Middlebrook Street.

The north-eastern corner of Winchester with the old Spitfire bridge and the Winchester bypass on the bottom left of the picture taken in the early 1960s.

Winchester's City Mill dates from 1744 and is the latest of many mills on the same site. It now belongs to the National Trust who purchased the mill in 1928. It has been used as a Youth Hostel since 1932 – the first YHA hostel to be opened in the county. The mill itself has now been restored to working order and is milling flour once more.

Winchester High Street when traffic flowed in both directions.

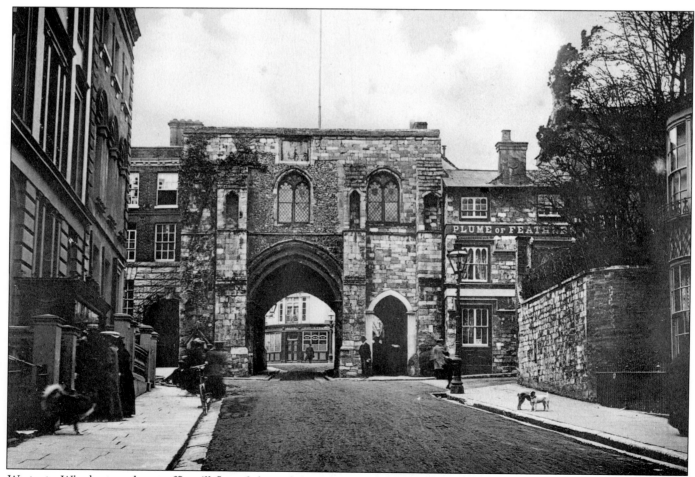

Westgate, Winchester when traffic still flowed through its narrow gateway. The picture is *c.*1900.

Bull Drove Swimming Pool opens – and despite the cool weather, young swimmers dive in. The pool formed part of the river that ran through it and was situated in Garnier Road.

Anti-racist groups march along Romsey Road, Winchester.

It's been many years since Winchester had a Labour MP but they are regularly elected to local councils. Here protesting members chat with the police.

No one probably misses this old building in Bridge Street, Winchester but the advertising hoarding brings back some memories.

The George Hotel at the top of High Street, Winchester, demolished in 1956. Barclays Bank now occupies the site and was opened in 1959.

The George Hotel in the process of being demolished. There had been an inn on this site since 1408 called The Moon. It was renamed The George in 1415 after the Battle of Agincourt.

Colin Cosier of Preston Candover constructed this wooden bike with the help of the village blacksmith who supplied hoops for the wheels.

The view from St Giles Hill, Winchester, possibly taken during the 1950s. The St Giles Fair was held on the hill in the Middle Ages and was revived in the 1970s. This view of the city is a favourite for photographers and TV producers alike.

Winchester's High Street in 1957. Timothy White & Taylors, just visible on the left, is now a video shop.

Wharf Hill, Winchester, being modernised. The grassed area in the foreground was the site of the Dog and Duck public house which closed in 1923 and was demolished in 1938.

Abbots Worthy Mill, near Winchester. Abbots Worthy is one of the 'Worthy' villages, the others being Martyr Worthy, Kings Worthy and Headbourne Worthy.

The new Barclays Bank built on the site of the George Hotel, which opened in 1959. The photograph also shows the widening of St George's Street and Jewry Street.

The building of Ashburton Court, Winchester, in the 1950s.

A warm water car wash for 2s 6d would be about 12½p in today's money, but still good value.

AND FINALLY...

31 December 1999 and crowds gather, despite the rain, outside Winchester Cathedral, to cheer in the new millennium.